*half* MYSTIC is an international, independent publishing house and literary journal dedicated to the celebration of music in all its forms. Half Mystic Press publishes carefully-crafted books of prose, poetry, and experimental work—invocations of love and wildness, the heartbeat of humanity set to a 4/4 time signature, expanding and redefining unsung narratives, sharp and lamenting, eyes on the horizon. For more information, similar books, and submission guidelines, please visit us at www.halfmystic.com.

# *Praise for Willows Wake and Walk Away*

"With elemental precision, Haley Wooning writes of aftermath and metamorphosis in language both earthen and ethereal—sharp as bone, soft as breath. The poems in *Willows Wake and Walk Away* do not merely describe survival; they enact it."

Sierra DeMulder, author of *Ephemera*

"*Willows Wake and Walk Away* is a book haunted by 'the plural of loneliness' in the aftermath of trauma. The 'dream-crazed' and grieving speaker of these lush poems—attuned to the mysteries of the nonhuman living world—asks, 'What endures?' In her search for a fitting myth, she encounters 'no hero to conjure,' no epiphany. In this poetry collection, what endures is the astonishment of having survived, of belonging to the earth's ever-changing songs."

Patrycja Humienik, author of *We Contain Landscapes*

"Positioned between root and rot, beauty and violence, 'ghost-lives' and bruised bodies, Haley Wooning's brilliant *Willows Wake and Walk Away* is built on ruin and recovery. We follow the narrator across night-dazzled landscapes of phantoms, bones, and forest animals, through unnamable losses where grief is 'a lyre that waits unstrung' to a reclamation of voice. Though loneliness, trauma, and survival are intricately knotted in these poems, the collection offers something other than despair: a tender hand reaching out in the dark, a stay against sorrow and harm. This is a book to return again and again for solace and the reminder that 'when the rot is through, the flowers will consume it.'"

Simone Muench, author of *The Under Hum*

FIRST PRINTING, NOVEMBER 2025
HALF MYSTIC PRESS
www.halfmystic.com

COPYRIGHT © HALEY WOONING 2025

EDITED *by* DANIE SHOKOOHI

ASSISTANT EDITED *by* COURTNEY FELLE *and* LEE ANDERSON

COVER ART *by* ANNE SIEMS
DESIGNED *by* TOPAZ WINTERS

ALL RIGHTS RESERVED

You know the drill. No part of this publication may be reproduced or transmitted in any form or by any means—electronic, print, photocopying, recording, information storage and retrieval, or use in training artificial intelligence technologies—without prior written permission from the author and Half Mystic Press, except for brief quotations in critical reviews.

Don't steal art. Authors need to eat too.

ISBN-13: 978-1-948552-18-9
ISBN-10: 1-948552-18-3

*For Sarah and Grace*

*Willows Wake and Walk Away*

Haley Wooning

A Half Mystic Press Publication

*Part I*

I do not believe in before.
the world was mute
and fat on indifference,
the fallacy of recognition.
on that field, nothing
familiar remained—
that rust-gnawing thicket,
that hinge-cry of bones
scattered by otherworldly winds.
they squeaked over fields empty
as I am. they had already happened,
the years I spent crouched in corners,
voice-fled. I was helpless against
language's unpossessable fragments.
the dark webs strung up in the night-water,
scoured like rot over the moon-colored
snout of earth. where did I go?
where were the hounds?
survival, lost time, the thrum
of days forgotten. what else was there?
I did not sleep.
I watched muddy lakes swell across the sky
until even eternity disappeared, murked
with gods' bloodied fists.
they struck, shattering everything.
beneath them, my life's
frail ribbons fluttered and dispersed.
somewhere, a breath taken and held.
somewhere, autumn yoked itself
to drowning.

it took so long. I sat, terrified,
in the moment that would not end.
now I wait, fused to the body,
its scoreless thicket. there was no magic but
ending. it ended,
it goes on. I wait.

There's no room for illness. I am stitched with trauma's stiff thread. I wilt into sorrow's weapon, too weak to foster blows dealt by wind. This is what life will do, madden the cypress trees with echoes. Fix me like an ornament. Dawn protrudes, exposing winter as a corpse slung over the hill's chilled shoulder. Mist crowds out the peering eye and those that follow must follow heedlessly. I want time to happen all at once, for the terror to pass quickly. In my hand, a writhing jewel, things I took and forgot the origins of. Was I ever beautiful? Did I age well? Dream-crazed, I slip into the haze, packed off into the black on the backs of phantom horses. All moves towards some gloom I don't recognize. All is forked tongue, all is blue dusk-light. What is this, then, now? No place at all. I must gather and put to words what evades me.

Dreams paralyze me. I pace the darkened ruins standing marble-masked and dull as death. The moon expends her waters across the night's unseeing mouth, white as degloved fingers. I walk, caught in tedium and waiting to wake. Each desire is a gnawed rib, pointlessly interred, waiting for the fabled stirring. The wind howls my terrors nameless; even the earth forgets their voices. I don't recognize them. Shouldn't I? When I move, they dress me in shadow. My gown is a rumor of all I've lost. The ruins crumble in exhaustion, weakened by time, and answer no questions. I love their thrumming emptiness. I rifle my feathers in their lifeless eyes. Somewhere, I am seen.

I forgot so much:

the sea's sigh, the owl-hollowed bough,
                the dull dim dumb thumping of hope
    in the heart's
                    splintered prow

the past became        unapproachable
             and now

I have little to offer
in votive,            a lamp once lit
    will gutter
    out

here is a temple no one visits,
            water turning stagnant
            and murked
in the sun
    of deserted castles

a name was once marked on this stone
but perhaps I dreamed it

the day I died I went into the dirt below
where worms
wait out storms
in wetter weathers

regardless of my want, the earth
remained murky and locked shut

for seven years I knew only
my own wintering,
worms wedding
the flesh

and wolves
that gnawed my ankles with false purpose
        stay and be good

is it not enough
to survive once
and so briefly?

I clawed their teeth from me
like wings torn from dying
waterfowl

The weaving is impossible. My narrow attempt flails, frayed and tameless. I'm used to labor. Those seven years I carry with me like a fever, voiceless and unnamed. I was a child when he found me, an adult with a stolen childhood when I left. Language escapes me. I shrugged off cruelty as I gazed from shadowed corners. It was only survival. There is no articulation. The gashed-out mouth of a moment. The blows landed forever. Don't look, look away. Who can speak of such times? Why must I? Why must I name it? Naming is another blow to suffer. Instead I speak of survival. Let me look. I am the gaze in the face of horror. Trying and failing to decipher and communicate. To relay what I witnessed and see still, even so much later. It will be another failure.

I left and never went home. I'm not the mythic figure with a home to return to. I have nowhere. I left somewhere. I would not return. I never did. It stalks me still. In my new realm I look in the mirror and it is uninhabited. I speak to the wall and no sound occurs. No one hears me. Where am I? Where did I go in my leaving?

cold spots freckle the shadows where
stars unmark themselves, ravenous
below a gazeless sky: here is water black
with ambition, torn
by arrival, a phantom threading
lusting over scattered stones

nightly I walk among them, an orchid
dulling its own brief color if only to be
lit once in the passing eyes of their strangeness
see me, I beckon
but speech is perennial and every gesture
abyssal and estranged

they do not heed
the stretched pale palmskin
laboring over each shadowy field scarred with
self-embalmed stars

oh, sorrows
in this infinity
I cast myself into the woven caves of wounded
dreamed-of magics

I stand at the field's
frozen mouth where the veiled
thistle takes on terrible
proportions. the loam is always
hungry. small deaths feed it:
frail bones of forgotten animals,
dried insect husks snuffed out
below mindless, plodding feet.
I watch an empire fade across
the dirt's smeared lips. I am afraid of the world.
the worms that converge
alone in shadow. just like that,
I will not be missed. food
for the gut of greater things. memories
no one can count on,
they slip
through me like a name
through time
written nowhere.

I am a blurred landscape
the last
sad grass                    in a lost meadow

how long for the veil to lift? lethargic
as woadsmoke
redwood         rioting lichen's confusion

I'm entranced by the dark soil's sway like
frays of nightingale threads stolen from the branch

no one living remembers their song

my hands are ordinary objects
pitiable as a shut door
hinge's cry

facts are not sacred,
nor their cruelties

the shroud persists, anonymity thickens
warm wax on the weeping brow
of some pyre-bent beloved is buried
absent, never seen         remains

I crouch below the poppies, their
swollen tongues lolling with pearls
the size of misunderstanding

they scatter the field like breath, and I,
forgetful as rain, tie their
stems bent by wind and animal
plotting. what endures?

all the tarnished metal hues,
all the songless trees

am I the feeble arms holding
all this dark?

I am precarious, knit into thick-barked
tree-limbs, even
insects break from me

I can't accommodate
        the moon's dozing consolation
illuminating the bloated
        waterlogged corpse of
individual fault

she passes and repasses,
impermanent

For so long there was uncertainty. Everything was a question, a dismal seeking. I gave it up long ago, but it lurks, a forgotten hope, a stain. Like this dusk or the next. The horrible repetition, the same leaden weight. It teaches nothing. I escaped. Can't it be that simple? The root was narrow, unfurling.

The dream had gone. The well was empty. I didn't know how to tell the difference. I lived this way: ushering the frailty of survival into each black-beaked minute. Estranged, I lived this way. Bags packed and emptied and packed again. Every voice, every doorknob a terror. Darkness encountered. I lived this way, but hardly, glossed ill with membranous midnight. Irredeemable injury. Easier to lie. I packed myself into corners. I made myself small, pitiable as a mouse.

Autumn came. I woke. I had lived too long without casting a shadow. Someone carried me over the threshold. Who was she? She who carried herself on thinning shoulders. Who escaped. Who barely survived. I look back and slump into deeper-fed organs. Do I live there still? In that time and cruelty? I don't recognize the glance and place of now.

I hardly lived in the before. There was no song or voice for me. I learned nothing and I escaped. Someone carried me. Come clear of the shadow, hero. You won't be nourished by history for long. Already I forget you. Or was I only ever you, or you I, or none of us at all?

the stars shed their serpent skein
along the shore, a mimicry

across the length of night's mirror
        my life unspools like a thread

with the weight of disregard
I slough off into mythos

damasked by time
the field dims

nothing more grievous than the weight
of isolation, moon-starved, haunted and
hung from the bough in which my eye
is mangled

meanwhile the world forgets magic

I sleep, a welter of wet leaves,
my head weighed
                          with their rustling
mournful, once
        I understood them
                  and now
                          only hunger is left

a gown composed of lifeless planets, the deaths of
small things that build and build
and become me

autumn, darkwood, nighthag
swoop down deft
on bitter wings

the heart's black swan is wrung
by the neck, unfleshed as the bone
that builds a woman's cage

these hands have finished their
kneading, if only to pause
for a thought     over ancient waste

I want to unlearn
the world

to keen and wail for the depths
buried, unburied, abandoned

october breeds a wine-hued sea, nocturnal hills
        wild with mist-heath and wolf

between this second and the next
my name turns against me

a final abjection,
the heart shivers like a creature torn from its flesh,
tender now or never: home a hush below
the surface
        of where once rivers, now loss,

piled like autumn gourds, deep uncanny
mine of tongues shorn from the woman's woodwork

        a useless begging
for shrouds wrapped around sprites of bark and rue
rot it all, all will rot

the violets will wither in the lap
and the whole horizon will shrink for them

I became a corpse-dragged pond, my mouth shaped
with other mouths, thought blanched
to bone with ravening sorrow-bred horses
going elsewhere, undestined

body, scrape of funerary mourners, walking
the trail of woven blue thread
and nothing as grave as that dusky annihilation,
to embark one desire with another, to want
that which keeps one from wanting

lit so low below the ink,
I might fathom such mists to forgive
the lies I was told

I arrive and feel orphanhood among the trees

bleached, unknown, imbalanced
kneeling and null to water bloodied
with an impossible, unaccountable past

I'd rather not leave my stain
but I don't have a choice          an ensnared animal

caged to earth's loneliness,
some throats fill with its gutted rot
others lean toward softer, false language
the past begs its own forgetting

in the pit of intimacy, I writhe like opaque
worms left to festering sun, knowing well
the soil, the distance beneath

the selves I never wore and dropped
like low burdens along the way, remnants
I seek now
in the desolate part of the belly where hopes
branch their skeletal fingers between
ribcage and heart: all this I would give
to revoke what I once was

I gave up on assurances—
the dark-eyed bog-mare watched
and waited

only gutted tree bark
spoke plainly

the rest, herded into uncoiling
wonder, the moon above
a dragged corpse

wrapped in tedious
cerements where desire could not
find her

I weighed it all
and my hand retreated
damp
and empty

is there another way to be alone?

I tire of this need
to write, cruel as a lover's gesture
interred below
the irreversible slide of
a dragon-mouthed sun

no language flowers there,
the rue between thorns

I blink slow as stone,
old as myth—
what wind will come
to collect me?

all my hours I spend married
to shadow
I must believe
in the hero's return

what comes after survival? my life
left behind me like a death, so
much lost time I don't know what
to do with

over the years my longings labored
before abandoning themselves like stones
dropped in black waters

dread to dread, I am
silent and fused
to the field, its loneliness

a mist I pass,
crouch my way through

is this survival, then?
a phantom among so many ghost-lives

a useless call to
the hounds that never
came, that never existed

I was sent into existence, passing over
a temporal sluggishness. slow down, it said,
your smallness forgets you

and yet I went on

disregarded below the mist-wraithed wound,
on moonlight I fattened
and fled
into the woadsmoke of dragon's breath, a wreath
made of fables and each brief respite I eked
out from my life's unreality

was it enough to be unknowable? the air turned thick
and murderous, each conviction something to fear

it is hard to admit the world was unkind

that the hunter was never real, that no one
could save me, that I understood so little

alone in my blood
fated as organs
tethered to liminal
blue threads

I am grief
vast and imprecise as morning,
when I arrive
truth is nowhere

nightly I witness
an animal wind
distill flowers
into earth, asking
nothing in return

who picks at these petals?
they furrow
collapsing where

I alone regard them with pity

petals as white as palms
and impossible as a name, its voicelessness

a bruise that, lit once,
steps from the room and is forgotten

woad, roan, rowan            tell me how to love past
            thickening anonymity
cold grave                  loss of distinction

I was tricked              downward into
the spellward mirror, where selves, like rain,
                  are lost beyond
            their brief occurrence

did I ever speak? my voice a web of smoke that strokes
the pane of fathomed cauldrons

I cannot say: this harms me
and my hands
        already tarnishing
flickering away

what strikes the water and
is nothing at all?

manipulation or desire
        if I could I would claw
it from me, bear it            no weight

it is horrible to discover a longing

unsheathed as wind and
vanished beneath
the dream's slick-slack
sad weight

possessed by lilies, tempests
sickened by solitude, everything
weighs too much

like a fate one can't help but mar
and let slip
        away

where is the water of
vanquished rivers?

this is a necessary illness, this apropos of nothing
seasighs and petals burgeoning from gestures
never made

grief, a room no one enters and I,
a limited and ordinary object
gathering in the corner of someone
else's home

I am alone at language's orphan-root
everything has an edge to it
hounds-tongue in the forest,
the dull recollection of yellow teeth from
nowhere's dirt,
touch-swallowed attempts

I did not
love well enough

forgetful as a fossil,
my body yields to a continent of stone
withered and sallow like a moon that lights
briefly the names empires lose
in their collapsing

I do not speak,
like grief, a lyre that sits and
waits unstrung, healing takes
a long time

deprived of ambition,
my fingers itch with passing seasons
the knowledge that nothing stays

the universe is not infinite, it has
an edge to it, whatever passes beyond
that final boundary will never
return

I see it all, foolish and dauntless
as the hike of ants up the hill winged by dusk
and animal hunger

I am no different, I lap like a river at any full moon-milk,
howl out the hollowing black beneath the mirror
I breathe water and flee
with paws, slip against
narrow insectness and speak no more

harbor this season with me, the grub-pale berries fatten
among the moldering leaves where my hands open
and shut like idiot petals
what labor will learn them? I eat my way out, throat
by throat, yet freedom eludes me

when the sun disrobes it is damnation: I am an albatross
of regret, the little else of leaf-littered gloom,
there is no pit to slouch toward, no shadow to marry

clatter-clash, the geese-like gestures love makes
when unseen

I left a year ago. Some days it is an eternity, others no time at all. One morning I woke and recognized the cage. My bruise-mottled arms incapable of warding off his violence. It wasn't fantastical, the leaving: no moonlit horse drew me far into the night, my belongings in a sack over my shoulder. No heroes passed through my door, armored, weapon drawn. No gods whispered in pools of murky water that I was worth rescuing. Nothing saved me from my own myth. I walked out of it alone, silent and creeping. Only I, and time, seeping like flux from a wound. I left behind my bed, my cat, my parents' wedding photo, decades I deemed proof of life. The door shut behind me. So much I did alone, didn't I?

Unfold a certain way and it all aligns. I survived. What do I do with my life, so long withheld from me? I passed as a ghost from the old world, gnawed down to fleshless bone, and into a new home where I recognize nothing. Whatever held me has fled.

It is winter. It is spring. I probe imagination's small bones, the rotting wounds of all I surrendered. The myth I fled from, backward and alone into nowhere. I fight not to disappear entirely. It is summer, it is autumn. Birds fuel the trees, in beauty or carnage.

I sleep alone with my questions. Solitude's grim dignity. When I wake, they disperse into dawn, forgettable fledglings. I am a creature of days, of minutes. Where is next?

I went
alone
down where
the copse of oak trees
released their last
dark apparition,
sloughing off
old flesh
into long and hidden
rooms

it became a maze,
roving howl and wood
or night like entrails poured
into earth, a worm bidding
that crude wait—I should
have looked away
I could not, I
wanted too badly
to see
myself

so I plucked my
eyes on the red branch
like an unknown verb, my
finger's webs dream-
culled: I split, I did not
look away, but in no
kindness did my life
open

and so I
spilled
into the sea like ink
moon-dragged and
deathless, I was
not mine

wild thing or woman? no,
pond of corpses

that liminal, fleshy sideways
sloughing
        into shapelessness

caught in the net of stark, roan
winds—I am another hoof turned loose
in sorrow

upon which loss has piled
and piled

mountain or cerement?
a twisting nightmare maze,
a dead-root, a silenced lyre

even the moon hunts
and wastes me

over the black murk of time's waters,
an illness inhabits my solitude
vast and imprecise as mourning

all this work, to feel unmoored
to forget the strain of language: who
else would I speak to? something

unknowable rots in the body
and does not heal

hillock, hill-wept billow
sorrows bellow below
the godshorn lands hacked
with violets, black-mawed
and crushable
as lament

I winter there
where heroes, mangled in the
doorway, pale
beyond understanding
and nick themselves nameless
on failure's inconsolable star

slow, the self's stark
        dolorous tree, unraveled
by the immaculate wings
        of strangers. I madden
with obscurity,
        with questlessness

though I want for something,
I know no belonging
        contrived simply below the spectacle
of a moon-snout dusk

do I hear the woodland's collapse
or is it just the weeping animals?

water leaves
behind
no memory

nightmares return swaddled
like the dead drifting aimless

all my hopes shift,
a tragedy of constellations unmoored
beyond another unforeseeable edge

I am no drowsy root, I gnaw and gnaw,
my fingers itch with want for unseen countries,
the blossoming soot of time

for all my longing, nothing is called

too bewitched by the old wound that,
like all else, can't recall
its own hanging

noosed and lifeless
back and forth
within me

thicket, sorrow-wheat
        perish here among the tomb-thick
attachment, the earth is dark
as meat as dark as     a hero's
fate unsung and
        hideous     how many disguises
have I worn? how many strangers
        in me have I forgotten?   nothing
is illuminated, a crow's waltzing shadow,
        the future's flowers pale beyond my reach

I pluck nothing
but delusion from
the heart's distended fallow

I've thought about freedom. Held its pulsing flux. The perennial reach of its fingers, distended and aching and sweet. I pass between them—phantom or hero? It doesn't matter anymore. I want to halt my own splitting. Into time, into selves, into unknowable space. I am the plural of loneliness, even now. Suffering halts time's meaning. And if I should mourn it, I don't know how. I would rather forget.

I can't understand the earth's capacity for simultaneity. Cruelty, tenderness. Isolation's incurable domain. Heroism never existed. Even sisters see what is lacking in the other, as all lovers do. As the self multiplies, bloats and seeps, the old one rots behind it unburied. I pity them, all that I was and was not. All I did not dream or dreamed too late. I'm here, and I don't know what it means. I feel my separation as a hook, the past gnawing at the present, a slip of the future, all unreal and pitiable.

I walk backward into my own story, gaze out, gaze in, gaze skewered on the callous spear. The world goes on, a spiral of black feathers. A sky severed down to spine and sinew. First comes shame, then duty. To survive, to upend. I am liminal, powdery, crumbs found in the creases of things. I forget it all, I forget nothing.

longing alone carried me through mist-dragged pastures,
through the dozing wood where roots like cold arms
tried to trip and hold me fast. I was hardly real,
a wizard's time-plucked
bone, a sigh of lost legends.

I walked slowly here, each dawn as forgettable
as an egg slipping from a child's fist into murky waters.
distant and cold as memories of the dead. what was
the wanting? nothing but the pull
of my feet, dark as roaches.

once I asked the world: tell me my name. there is hunger
in hope and, like all else, it is tired. the grass was a grief
beneath me, sluggish as the grime on old village bowls,
fattened on milk's inevitable rotting. I was
lost but somewhere I entered

gutted by indifference, wordless as a cupboard. I was
committed to live, for however long. what would I make
of it now? the ruin of flowers behind me,
                              my dream's ill use.

it begins—

I wade,
flush and dim,
crossed by
the misunderstanding
brought on by ambition
and its ruin

the godless tide falters,
like the notch of an
arrow I have nicked
the fabled lung

what bleeds out
I cannot say

I believe
the water belongs to me
and my loneliness
fallible

somewhere
I will remember
I happened

after centuries of sleep
I wake. like opening the mouth
of a grave, not even the wind will look

gravity caught in sorrowful
cinders, blooming and bleeding,
a strange continent

in my mind it is autumn
the trees droop and
weep their leaves like
so many wrinkled limbs

and I am less lonely, confused as
everyone else

a hinge below memory's
depths, I haunt with impossible
wanting—

no, I wake, it's winter and
I am bent bones holding up a brief body

suddenly and with quick violence
I realize the roughness of my hands

who would hold them? pitiable as the weeping
door hinge that opens into nowhere

kingdoms are forged then effaced by passing
moons, as frail as joy or dust or lilies

the slow mounting illness: I see I am alive
and given to the terror of knowing

swathed in curse, paws forbear no remembrance
I am like that, I think, curled into quiet dens
and murmurs of my own brief wanting

night as cold and sharp as winter's garden

I am so frail alone
a slow unspooling from blue bones
into unmarked dreams

they flicker like cinders, in and out like
the consciousness of muddled animals,
and where

is consolation? hounds-tongue in the forest,
everything with an edge

where the moon rises, a wreath of flaxen
light blooms cutting serpent-shapes across
the sea

this is the world I touch, am defined
and named by, but I'm looking for
a lighter sorrow to shelter

I touch the world's weight,
a blossoming blue
language
startled like birds from low grass

only the meadowsweet consoles me

here is the fever of fumbling, dreams planted
beyond their syllabic furrows where villagers
wet their snouts into
harvests lost; I will my own plainness

it takes little urgency, the woodland's door
sways open, empty
of understanding

no one will warn me
not to look—
I'm alone in this
estrangement like a fern uncurling its
frail bird-neck for the ax's
clumsy tumble

dark cud, mouths maw on
whatever war-hewn
mud the earth has left to offer

whose bones are these?

dark as the inside of nowhere

furrows where nothing is planted
and each creature, succumbing
to wind,
        finally nestles into sleep

all these years my body's dirt waited
worm-weighed, peat-worn,
a winter dream cast off
from dulled hooks

I empty out my old hopes,
they clamber like fey bells
in a breeze
        far away

new things come
        glancing into
places where abandoned creature-bones
rattle emptily in their husks

here, everything is ending
the heart, white and sickly, no longer
intractable
        cannot be lost for good

mid-drowsy root, fawnhoof
dragon's tail clovering the ground like perfume

I had so long forgotten wanting

a dead god's statue sits
stoic, unseeing as sun

who made these ruins? aimless
as night-dazzled tongues
stretching
each distance while
my grasp reaches and
returns with mist

below me, dragon-scales sepal the water,
fathomless ships drift, unmoored by time—
I know language is lonely work
and violent as it tries
to dig up      or resume
      lost rumored ores

unrecoverable        hope is
a lily, musk-thick, leaning in the dark near
the coffin
where the eye cannot tread

must I find new words
for love?

I, lone traveler, carrying night heavy in my hair
snag like mist over bog, moon-sick and tenuous

the wrist I plucked like a petal from far away fields
sinks to the bottom of the sallow waves, becoming
the apparitional drowned of my dreams

who among us can recall affection? I age,
croned with peat-black hair; my childhood's palm
unfurls and loosens its secrets

like wind, love goes elsewhere

and the planet, alone as a spider's husk,
starves silent into itself over and over

grief is a rot in the blood
with mud-weighed feet     I pass over nothing

I came shrouded
out from where rivers
ran once, those forests
borne of mist and
dread

would the animal,
lonely, prefer another
kind of ensnaring?

the distance is
perfumed in
longing, how sad
a small song

torn
another woman's
exile, intangible

willow, wisp, smoke
or ash the haze
surrounding

a heart's dense
unutterable
night

the world
as dark as stars hung
limp over the
rot of old gods

I have heaved my own
spirit behind me, her weight
was too changed
and disconsolate

I was too tired of
abstractions, tracing out
the dark that continues to

shrink and lift
the stone below
its thumb pressed
down as rough and
tameless as ruin

I wait, my tongue
swallowed by unseeable moons

I don't know how to
forgive myself of anything

the sprouting
crabgrass and crude-cut
worms
  languish and slip
like gowns from ghostly shoulders

one forgets they are human
that we live outside our dreams,
those green, forbidden woodlands

sorrow is a consequence

wasn't I told not to
  speak
of things
  intangible as wind? I am

that, aren't I? forgettable
as a feather a meager mortal
thrum or am I

a reed bending
pitiless  shaped from another
time? one I
do not recognize or am
capable of conceiving

loneliness makes a
stagnant hollow sound,

    a song that forgot
the sea or
    a song the sea
forgot

I fail at everything, a myriad of dissonance
wormwood sighs and stars unlit by
a god's loveless handling

my dreams skip like stones
over pale waters with
        prey's parting murmur

ineffable
moons rise over the edge
of this sorrow

I slope along
        the wolfhills
nightdrenched
        and deranged

I am fathomless
and strange

the scent
of spirit consumed

or the mist
        obscuring the
edge of a
midnight water

no purpose in
lying anymore

I will tell you what
I know

I never ask
the right questions

I collude with shadow
where even the earth can't see

in words never spoken, gestures
never made—in dreams I forget
to dream until it's too late

my life is a closed well, I have
seen too much, my eyes are shut
in sea-flowers

that bloom with tethered stars, they
are like fate, neither here nor there and
never mine

too much, the weariness of distance,
the perfume of those false, final sensations,
that an end would come

that there is a realm, in itself, infinite
and composed, having already lost
that power to console me

and so, consoled by nothing, known
by no thing but untraceable twilight
gardens where the sea sounds

a memory of my churning fingers,
governed beyond their own contradiction
or that tapping, tender fawnhoof

only the fool believes they can bear anything,
that exile could be like sleep, partaken and
consumed, forgotten come morning

I am where isolated things belong

each day I'm
drowned with
imagination
the gaping
maw
of prayer

the earth yawns, what is shut
will not open, a serpent snores
below the sea

taking from me what
time is bound
to take:
memory, affection

I slouch
down
into the dawn-depths,
a life possessed
by distance

the waiting for hands

where I step, the water darkens
the bloated body slips
and spreads
between
the seams,
frail and colorless
swans

they bring in their wings
to die

I've given up
on pacing, I see now only the night-touched
sea and her legion of ageless,
fluttering stars, lost
to the tide's moonlit gown

lapping lipless on the languished shore,
this, now that, now nothing

I bore myself with my own repetition
but I don't yet know how to be different, something
that lives beyond nostalgia or the musk
of a forgotten half-life. do I remember
being a daughter? memory
is a moth shorn of wings,

throttled limp and faceless.
the daughter cannot be good. she has
strayed too far, misremembered

the unforgivable whispers of pooling dew
like the stains
of stars, a slaughter-gush of
scarlet blood, tears. we are all meat and split-soul.

wasn't dawn supposed to be saffron-robed and
numb with mortal lovers? this,
now that, now gone.

every river pales beneath the great graze of sleep
like a rampant hoof the night has fallen, it will not rise
again: everything ends here

I have fallen
so much rain
upon the world's standstill
gesture

the milk is tinged with blood where the mask
is drawn out by coarse needles—am I
tongue or eye?

I wait to be told how to discern oneself, depths
below and nowhere at all, I wait to be a still lake,
corpseless,
carved in the calm, mewing chord

to be sounded, or unheard: one makes for more glory,
more redundant desires of a cruel and
fable-fingered god

I shaped myself in this space
displaced by absence and alone

tossed like mindless god-hewn waves,
I prefer grief to nostalgia, its thick-mawed smoke that
towers and peels back tough flesh to show—
what? stains, pomegranate-red
ponderous and despaired along the dirt's stark surface
where I bloat, belly-up, in the field curdled with lilies and
dreams, so many
dreams of forests I can't see because
I haven't mended well enough—isn't this too
a cruelty? I am a horror; I scour
tar-black pots, my hands sour as old eggs
that trip and tumble over a wanting that turns
like fabled heroes into stone
even now what's left of my animal
is maned with it, moon-wreathed, knowing
no other
belonging
it is my name I wear and maim with

unspeakable as a weapon and more real

night-fountains of the mortal seam,
unbidden, forbidden, hoarfrost veiled
I touch the black herb of my soul's

dusky garden, unseated and dying now
as one creature into the next, tethered
to twilight's soft waves

and the parables of a cave, my crossroads
where the wolf is beloved by water
then drowns, enchanted
by the indifference of stars

and nothing else: the otherworld's flute
plays and plays
forgotten
        by all but me

the treading ferns of language go dim
as if it is a tomb that has spoken

as if it is skin weighed
with the lost while
the mind does not realize

the blue threads that tie
it down

how could it be so final? dark forests
breed myths into mist. I need more time.
cold, cruel pacing hour, the whole world
shut like a fist squeezing the last threads
from a wound. I am alone, only
my own.

the stars, like bodies forsaking love,
pass over the night's water, a phantom
mist, another bone to bury

forget me, this is the hour where I plunge
strangely and perfume the forest

the moment, a suspended blade
I bring down on the thread tethering me

to all other things—is this what
survival looks like?

It's something like the thrash of death. Or grief.

My flesh abandons its old wounds. No doorway holds me, nothing looks on with a pitiful eye. There is no hand straining at my throat. No violence to bruise my arms against. No need to hide. My life flows everywhere now. I learn new words for freedom, though my mouth feels nonsensical and small. My feet carry me. Fairytales are not real and reality grounds me. How simple these new joys are—how unfamiliar, how I still learn them. What does the body forget that the self won't?

I humiliate myself and eat it all. Bones. Memory. Language where language is not. I waited a long time and nothing waited for me. After recognition comes voice, comes terrible longing.

Old life. I hollow you out below the thumb of Now.

*Part II*

night disobeys, but fog is compliant
turning an animal eye on the fringe
of my strange, lulling sleep

that witnesses both love and the wolf, the water
crowded with broken ships and the ancient plagues
that populate them like
unknown birds singing heedless of themselves

they hold that lonely look,
the edge of something forsaken and far off

where I have walked too long, shaping cathedrals
out from my own longing below the sea

when it distends and floats belly-up, will it be
eel-pale or blue? the shape of another death
bright in my dark ignorance

how terrible it is, that moon moored over
those lost memories that refuse
to be mine

the world is ever in flux and unknowable,
winds shifting and sifting

dirt over my heart's pointless ruin
becoming more like worms and mud and winter,
someone tell me what it means

His fingers, round and pale as grubs, held fast. Below my feet, the world turned. A year later, I wake dream-weighed, recalling too sharply the touch of it. I remember the minutes that built those years and a grave opens below, salivating. This is articulable, tangible as a bruise; it is all I have. Easier to say *this hurt me* than to express years of violence with nothing else to hold. What it is to live so many years already-lost. To lose any romanticization of survival. To trace the aging skin and say: *this is time stolen from me. For so long I did no speaking.* Haven't I reclaimed it? My life, this voice? Why, then, the waking in the past? The losses are unnameable. What use recovering them? It's easier to grieve the physical. I would rather the brief flashes of a hand at my throat, here and gone, the bruise left behind, than the haunting of the irretrievable, irreparable, impossible gone. It is so much of me. Isn't that why I'm here? To reclaim something of myself. To discern the nature of hell before building a fortress on its precipice. It is hideous work and it is mine.

night's seduction is infinite, unknowable
and remote as the stars—what's next?
her tresses swept with hunger? I see them
now, their gaze hard, torn from the wings
that once bore everything

what god planted them there, faceless
among the bare trees, crueler than
a thorn in its hidden lurking? I'm like that,
I think—but perhaps I just want to be
anything, perhaps
there are some myths that, by naming alone,
shift their victories to failures

I tell myself I can bear anything
winter emptied of trees
or spring fueled on ashes

each of my wakings is strange,
each dawn I am plunged into mist
upon phantom wings

still, I move on—I forgive the quiet
assertion of graves—
if I saw the sea again, would I remember?
even now, my senses dull and flail, I am
patterned in the inconceivable reach
of stars: each an abandoned kingdom

here is my desire for goodness, it is
an annihilation; for the rest of my life I
will forget and keep forgetting
how then, tenderness? the core stalks
us everywhere, madness is not a thing
with color, blanched as meat in hot noon,
yet it protrudes in each direction

easier to secure like rope my body with images—
a huntress, the moon, hands besotted with swallows
and wolves stalking the omissions black with time
in my mind I watch them fill the field with sound,
I must keep them close to me, other longings are
crude and fruitless

somewhere, I changed; no use recounting when but
the hot mouth of their happenings: violence
or violation, my body bloomed pointless
below battered rain

here is my penance, I am a daughter's meat
bowed with fantasies, exiling myself
you, here, you're like me, and everything around us
touched pale with that weary extinction
I tell us: we have found the thing that is unbearable

how can I sleep
with internal lands
and language
so unknown?

I pulled these bones
from the sea,
mired my husk
over them

at first they were strange,
rattled by winds and the carved-
out dark of human weight

I split open like night, spilled
pomegranate or entrails—nowhere
the blue, everything
dispassionate, unfamiliar,
the earth cleaved by star and time

I evoked the waters, the well of
words never made, what I forgot
to dream marked my mouth with
elsewhere

do these passing, haunted faces
sense it? I am as quiet
as the illegible
statues that litter the corners
of abandoned hallways

once I cooled
like lead where wings drooped
their tethers in horror and skin
passed nebulous through the threads
of a secret world

every desire to be held: a cello or
a woman's voice on the edge of sound,
made impossible by the hands choked
and strained beyond it

I do not sleep, I hear
stairwells converging in ravens

the echo curling in on itself
to lick its sad, absurd wound

an animal in the last silent forest

each memory will toss a moon like a
coin into the nocturnal fountain and
will be lost there

so what use is my wakefulness
watching the ghosts cast
their untold wishes

before they stalk away
with no need to wait for answer

here is the indigo
and woad
       of privacy

strange how easily
we forget

how easily a worm begets
its earthen writhing
for metal
       or pavement

transfixed
by the ordinary,
the wind shapes
riders of myth
and ruin

sometimes I think
I hear them—or is it
my own feathers
that rustle and weep
wet
       and raven?

somewhere I gave up
I can't remember
when

nothing left
but the sea
      and my wanting

how long since I wrote of
      prowling wolves?

I look back and see only my own terror
that small, corner-crouched dark
      paltry hidden    cry unheard and
      pointless to recall

better the vain turning of moons
and noose and ribbons than
the urgent longing
      for substance
ingrained like runes into some hidden
forest fountain where the winds whip up
laments from ghost-mouths cut-gashed
loose and scarlet

what is this?
bloodied-animal or gnat just evidence
to know if it is mine

in my arm's realm
all this meets
I collapse

pity me

the field is alien, worried down to the weary-bone—

was it I who plucked eyelids like petals from the

unsleeping mud? I watched the crowds of death

pass by, obscured by mist. here is how one feigns

indifference: I held something deformed

and animal in my hands and inside its beating I

diminished. no one knew. no one noticed the world

dim between the field and its dream. or perhaps

the prints of arrogance will always remain. the long,

dusk-dark dance of impermanence. only

the thievery of belief, the field with its wedded

eyes, her animals numberless and indistinct, trailing

mist without thought. I, another swarm among them.

woods weep with willows
wrought by waning wants,
their waking will winnow them
away

dusk, dare I trace the bones you've eaten?
bloom with orphanhood's admittance,
the inevitable, soft dissolution

no hero is nursed by history for long
does everyone burn like this? hurried and gone

language held only by the sea,
whose labor is irreparable, tumultuous loving

I exhausted myself in the pursuit:
what will hold me now?

the whole world tires

between forest and monster a tomblike
dark reigns alone

I build its throne, maim the caves, slough
bones from the marred fields where my old
life's temple sits damp and ruined

alone in recollection, memories like so many
dark swans wrung by the neck and fleshed
from the echo of a woman's cage

I have so long held the fruit of voicelessness,
who could I tell? the roots, eons ago, stopped
their hushed speakings,

no more cloistering
trees to eavesdrop, no more phantoms
to scatter their wailings

no time here, suspended,
the body that never
quite feels human

I watch the blood pool thick
a scarlet-spray of dew

here, the blue snare
that waits in the dark

a frail net I cast
into the night

what drags back
is empty

how uncertain the distance,
the chest's black orchid

the suspended, dense swamp
splendid with tedium

I cannot
tell you what it is I hide

what footsteps I hear
parsing the blackened roots

in a landscape where tenderness once lived—
everything is arrow-nicked and
dulled into rot-soft fruits

I hide myself, there is no purpose,
no one to ask
after the remains I keep and bundle like
the bones of forgotten things

so it is being loved once and forgotten
my never spoken name jagged
        thick as rain-wet earth
in its puddles of dumb, jostling confusion

moonlight pools in my palm's plinth,
the color of pearl, nothing but
faraway medieval airs and castles scraped
to bare stone and dispirited in their ruin

yearning resembles hunger, hollowing
in its gravity and all I know
lies cradled in the dark branches of trees above, they are
ignorant of dusk, abandoned even by their own wanting

whose meaning is a lack of shelter, of light? amidst
the body's inevitable isolation, even fate turns elsewhere

in this way I lose myself in fantasies
devoid of revelation

I have become myself, stranded,

        crude and cut as a worm gorged

on murder. poor fruit, once glimpsed

and easily forgotten, you are

dull and needless

        as my longing. for

what? the red crisp-crunch of bones

mawed over by wolves and winds thrashing

        unknowable musings. I don't look

away. there is always loneliness

to witness, its own animal.

        a shade's wallow. let

me bury these moments. empty of me. small,

slow-fading pulse of living.

divined by shadow the roots

slip drowsy half-dreams

      curled in cold clay

under the wet

      match of my name

the wind, absentminded,

empties the trough of me—

horses glare

      wildly unfettered

when only I

      would sing to them

who is left to

      peel from the hour the

madnesses' dull glaze? how

numb it is, snagged by

       such unknowing, only I

at the edge of the water,

groping alone for

       familiar shapes

small animals, my hands
colluding with shadow over night's ruin
breathing shapes into trees: this is
dawn's peril
to see what loved ones find lacking in the other

let it not be lit, let day never come
I who want nothing but myth and mist and wind
to be what I am not or where I
have never been

whose form am I in? I tread
sluggish as a marsh beast that slumbers below
starvation's threat

the moon is gold, large, a war in the russet of winter eaves
outside my window
        a suppuration
        what bellows below
black-mawed violet? here are the shadows that people
my fever. like the intimacy of freckles, I can't look away.

I've been alone too long. I forget the old lives
        passing, unpassing. the iron door shut.
the wound's raw meat bereaves itself elsewhere.
what have I made of myself?

I fashion earth into myth. night now and I'm paralyzed
by dreams. I pace their dark ruins. no one
is here—                        alone I move below
        stone figures made from lost kingdoms,
long-dead gods, monsters whose names I'll never know.
dull as a promise, they can't help me anymore.

night now. her waters expend themselves across statues'
unseeing mouths. I walk among the humble figures
caught in motionless tedium. their moon-gnawed ribs,
pointless and interred, wait for the waking of the fable.

will I name them again? how long before dawn pulls her
blanket over this swathe and they're lost?

each waking breath snuffs them out. the wind howls them
nameless. like them, I am the rumor of all I've lost.

I want to
        love them, weigh them. make them real
for the moment I'm not.

I lie in nights crouched
below, guttural

holding a thing
absent of recognition

relic or ruin? I will not
last forever, copseblue

nescient as twine

arrows scrape the landscape of some
anonymous wound

moth mullein clutch the field like knucklebones
gnawed fleshless by winterbent winds

I lean into them, a stain among gathered lives,
chimera fleeing her uncertain kingdom

unaware as midnight, each waking unrecognizable
as childhood, the place where the world tires and weeps

fabled heroes disappear, if they ever were

a once-home broken, inherited by an innocence
never allowed—this, survival, then?

my mind dull as pewter, snagged out by wringing
roots and hands—the blood no longer flows, just birds

maddened red to measure the last song, the weight
of inaction, another exile, untroubled by the doleful tree

fog on the edge of nocturnal water,
these grim woods
ring with stark, mothpale hands
that turn cruel with time—

somewhere     a blue moon wastes
and hunts me

somewhere     a god's thumb irons against
    the hollowing throat
no more singing in the dark

somewhere, once, far from now
I am a white thought blanched to bone,

the ravening maddened sorrow-red horse
undestined, elsewhere, alone
in the long, long wait for change

I unpetal poppies where the sun dares not
thread its lust. all dusk, I gather them to me like tinder.
the world gave me up. I shake
language loose like stars ungirdled over water.
dream of villagers mid-rot—I muddy them all
where I touch, hellebore moaning,
lies turned to carved
marble. nowhere have I written my name. no one
stops at my door. the solitude is ungovernable
and mine alone.

spring's arms molded with magnolia

an animal secludes itself, a single throat, and whispers
to the dark: I witnessed eternity

where I went I went alone

no one to cast pity on the stony palm of my errors
or ask how each smudge
of dusk expends like a sickly lung

no witness, no wish, no age, nothing for the world
to remember—when did I cast a shadow? when did I
know a fact not proven false? the footsteps, love's lure

embittered on the landscape of a window
never looking out; this room is my belonging
ghosts come and go, watching me flail
from life to life

the woods speak, the sky's armament disarms itself,
the earth is sick with the promise of the impossible

spring, you come

but my eye is shut
and I tire of fighting

nights I had meaning
brief as a body below the
breaking, black bread
of distant suns

I littered the crimson reeds
like something dreaming, but
still I was alone
silvered by spiderbled jewels
and vacant castle halls

feudal palm, I held the moment:
who else
heard the aimless tapping
in the crow's cry?

the sharp ache passed
then absolution
as if it never happened

like living
in a mirror, this saturation
of dreams from which there
is no waking

abhorrence is as natural as breath:
for language,
for language lost, for a reality
so singular and sheer it is impossible
not to witness its own futility

tonight I am cold as an eye rattling
gazeless in its husk
torn from even the want of knowing
the small, innumerable humiliations
it bears

I no longer name you, vision
sleep-feathered and sharp
the spirit's cruelest principle

the world emptied of whispers, dusk
sheer as wings unfurled where I lost myself
between mirror and fountain

no one saw me as I passed
a shade unshaped by shadow
a tether unraveling from
the plinth of the gone and forbidden

it was unkind of the earth to be silent,
to disparage history
in a moment: who bears remembering?

I was as purposeless and ugly as an orchid

the wind flayed my limbs, sent them
scattering to the fields

after so many endings, language abandons
even I, who begs and seeks
so rare and capricious a thing—was it
ever mine?

sad, torn shadow
part that was nearly loved
move now with languor
into dusk, disappear
beyond inviolable isolation

your pale body rots, I sense it
here, graveward, where ants roll
about their grim crumbs and grubs
fatten on curdled milks

deaths turns all
things anonymous

everywhere it thickens
what labor can distract me? the perennial
unburied corpse of my feeling
festers, touched with what cannot
be touched, its shadow
mute and dumb as hands held underwater

and one finds again that realm
beyond fantasy, dragon or twisted knight

burrows aching
choked with fallen weapons I pluck
like idiot petals

I let fall what will fall; shadows bend
and twist as coming-light looms

the thrum of wood: lonely as an autumn forest,
violet I curl under, pale as the moon's palm
her petals complain and drop, scattered by wind's
galloping-roan ruin

I watch ages recede into night's distance

grief dotes my brow, stippled with frost, a gooseflesh sky
I turn the song over, crimson leaf, what else is there but
expendable scarlet thirsting?

my blood feels foolish, my isolation
ancient and common

I belong with those sisters of hauntings
living in mirrors
the dream saturation from which
nothing wakes

I am sorrow-sworn
imperious
like a name clawed from a throat
passing this heather where
animals litter the shadows my hands cast

if I knew what was coming, what would
        I change? the ash-tree of my window
skirts the autumn breeze, suddenly
        and vaguely I am real

then the hour passes, lightless as eons
        even eternity disappears

I've grown used to
loneliness

doors that open
then close like the
mouths of wild
animals

what is the weight
of passion
unused?

I find no purpose
in them, the birds
that sing and sag
    wingless
from my shoulder

I am not
at all
a thing I
once was

the earth or I
too changed? the snoring
jealous sea serpent
moon-tossed and
ocher

I recall only the hoarfrost
dumb
deprived of eyeteeth

a voice too maimed
and mare-maned
to recognize ruin
damp or pointless

it is mine, somewhere I
know this

I worm my way
down

confuse for wolves
the shameless fog
through woads like
corpse-hair curls

I lose myself there

the insects buzz on
unaware of
my dread hollowing
the night

like an illness or
a longing
        busying
the tall grass, the lake
of invisible tethers

my body waters
its flesh as if
snagged in a well's blue
snare, a sapsick swelling

I was told secrets
fattened below these roots,
pluckable and within reach

but my arm's freckles
remain too far
I had to look away

lichen spills
from the pine like damp curls
of hair          and I

glance a thin finger along their
edge, beheading so many
wishes for flowers

lilies dapple dark dirt like lips pulled across yellow teeth.

the forest remembers me, erased by wind's artless fingers,

the realm of each haunted star. at the edge of blue, I sit

waiting for a passing glance to recognize me. I can't

conceive the doorway, each mouth confused by time;

they fade, become forbidden in the dusk. where I gaze

too long into the cauldron, the world unspools—

what have I ever known aside from its horrible peeling?

I am tired and don't want you anyway.

I thumb the wreath of my wrist and think how small,

how frighteningly fragile, hardly anything at all. I should

belong to wetlands, decaying castles, forests alive

with ghoul and fay. threshing freckle, songs. the weight

of a heart sloughing off its innumerable dead. the flesh

rots in the gut. slow and undivided. the moon,

both universe and body.

I know the songs
of lost kingdoms

I know I am shameful
        an animal soured beneath
its own sick sad
                slick-slack weight

inchoately plumaged, my
mouth seizes with
        rustling feathers

I wed blue with devotion,
my dowry like desire and
false as mist

a red mirror moon stoops
        a cold finger into night's water another
inconsolable dream while the stars
pulse and gag in distant vigils

even they stopped looking

*stop talking about it*

the life of a haunted thing,
occult-strained, knowing only
how to ask for scraps

the swamps and penance that beget
a dreamscape—if ever I was
let no one remember me now

the songs changed, the unspeakable
entered them,
rivers stagnate and snag the phantom limbs
that wail and reach into nowhere

never a home
I am
mutable as wax on stone

      so changed,
but I know you,
your palms two pomegranates
red and sweating

meanwhile
something fades, unrecoverable

gold fields asleep
and helpless
I learn my loss when I learn
there are no words for it

that nothing will be spared from
the world's black spade

what is this hacking, anyway?
a gift,
a poppy, nodding,
bent in the cruel hook of the sun,

morning
and more of me is gone

truth never arrived, the earth held
its breath without reason, an autumn
yoked to drowning: it took a long time,
the labor, the dwindling care,
I sat, terrified, and recognized the moment
when the door's the horrible maw gaped open
split crimson mouthed and
moved on, gorging on the next

I learned nothing from the deaths
that marred me beneath those hands as crude
cut as maggots
memories now, receding always
into night's ineffable distance
and nowhere certainty
it's finished

unlit, insects bear no gaze of resurrection
I am the depths of my own isolated night
galloping woodward, a mix of moonwave
aimless as the worm-wed cave mute with
the long, dull slough of longing

below, don't the stars flicker? the forest stands
stubborn, her cinderhewn trees black with last year's fires
I hoard the ash of their leaves
just let me save something
the irreversible dark slide of mouths over earth's ruin

the realms I write from, vast moons hewn down

everywhere the hunt for meaning
mire-smirched, wind-hallowed hills
this too I can learn to love

I was watching strangers,
how transparent they become
when in love

was I ever like that? obsolete
as I am, each mortal dream fled long
ago across the waters

how do I regard them now? pale,
threadless, but don't I also
blanket self-pity in mistake?

a cello raving alone
in the dark

flowers snap open
like jaws asserting themselves
from the void of a hunger

where my dreams hurry from me,
emptiness reigns
disguised

there is no hero to conjure or trick
into aberration

just this, the place where
dusk folds its wings and sorceries
forgotten to time mark between them
a final terror

everything that has ever been
is exposed like a rotting organ

when the rot is through, the flowers
will consume it

I dredge the dawndim sea, a void

        displacing the sky beyond the heath

where I wring my wrists and outgrow

        radiance. only sometimes do I recall

the terror of being alone, the red-crisp crunch

of bones that echoes

        my life. otherwise I remain

in sand softwhite like sleep, each small

        hour an isolated

silence. the stars visit, winged phantoms

tossed from far-flung corners

        of obscure worlds. nightly,

each arrogance, each memory of touch unfolds,

replacing human hoping. only sometimes

do they call my name, as if

      to keep me from forgetting,

to keep my ash-weighed eyes a witness: someone must

see them in the morning, that shrug of stars

      snuffed out

across the sea. who else will weep?

who else will wait

        to burn the last of all animals? I want

for nothing else. longing drained from me

like milk from twilight thistle. I am

what the world demands        woman

        lacking shape or voice

hollow as that

        flesh-torn smell of lilies. thick,

sticky-sweet. they try and fail

        to blanket the dying.

I did not belong to summer,
its troubling
stifling of hands, the body's crook, her starless
roots and nothing left to starve the isolation

each year I forget, I remember

the yellowed hills, spoiled organs, my details
that time gnawed down to the fruit-pit unspooling
now over the labyrinth's hushed bone

now to the fleshless essential,
rituals of exposure met between the toothless
gums of ancient gods; the sun bears no kindness

I pass below the wretched thrum, a heathen
waiting for dusk, her moonwan darklit landscape
where animals corner themselves into wounds

like the windbent whim of so many shattered lilies
I open their many mouths, broken in the stitching
of my arm, an invisible life unfolds

inconsolable, I hate the waking, the morning already
sweltered and colorless on my window

I plummet, I forget, I wait
for autumn, her hues of endurance
beyond which mends
the inarticulable

rending, rooks nook about the ruin,
lost as time
        I am witch-bleak,
wrought        by ceremony's absence

a mordant look no root can patch on,
        below the sky's gray gooseflesh
I need not speak of it—

from what field and fabled forest
        do I heave and rest
my head? my old life
falls away, witless as flesh

I mark each weeping forgotten
displaced
        by rumor's nest

gods lived here once, winds
whipped them nameless, and even this
was forgiven

what is constant? the next wind's arrival
devastating the spirit. bewitched by time's adder, I
silver the trees like so many spiders. I speak into
the world: I know what it is to be kind. to sleep
unlit below tremulous half moons, an animal unfurled
along the muted grass. being's mysterious, imperiled
edge. what does it matter? skin is always spurned
by the invisible. another exile, like waking,
like breathing in the gloom. everywhere the little eggs
of grief drop and splatter. no end to their labor,
like insects or stars. a visceral descent on language.
I had forgotten the origin of such violence. even now
I say and mean nothing. I sway aimless as woadsmoke,
vespers shadowed in secret incense, mindless
tendrils of some bygone wish. all this longing.

madness, are you my mirror or shadow?

my dream with blue feathers, torn now
as the wolf from a woodland

my occult bespeaks its wretched flowers,
forgotten winds so long unmourned

I must remember who I am without
sorrow, such war-red tethers

you unfurl in the gut of somewhere,
as if a hand, open, torn

midnight, black and roan, nightmares
loose in the ruin of my once-garden

all of this and more am I not, within the
tales two animals spin for each other

and just so, as a lover does, my history falls
away—small, lamentable petrel

how I will no longer know your earthen
rivers, nor beg forgiveness of the heedless copse

I'll be indifferent to all I have been, lay her
to the waters and leave her there: I follow

the course of this sea

in a musky, midnight-shorn dream

I descend into the maw of a blue cave

the crones wait inside, huddled in moss, hanging

tapestries from stalactites, dusting fog

with a wave from a bone-sharp shoulder, damp

ankles infinitely treading

some limitless sea

my lungs are weighed with

the foreign voices of women

ensnared and removed from their

longing to speech

here, now, disembodied

but alive, desperate ring of a dull bell

that lashes us to astonishment:

let the moon remove her fur and shadow,

let the last keepsake, small lapis stone, the sybil's

flickering and fragmented leaves

be sewn together, to call us home

nights I squat in the cornucopia of
my dream's dense ear—
infinite and cold as
the stone that builds far-off ruins

like this, I heave into being, married
to shadow, fattened on mist, I unspool
like thread over the black stones of longing:
I know what it is to be alone

but I fear no longer, rooting deep among
the grub-pale knuckles, skulls and bones
I recover my look of the sempiternal, so
brief I am yet the dark goes on forever

the month of harvest is ending, I am all mouth:
December is an absence and how
luxurious the silence is, built of centuries
having loved well enough, I—

Ships unmoored from the mist of my dream-making. I can get used to anything. My nondescript capabilities, the terror of belonging or loneliness. When the body goes cold, I remember it, swaddled in stories. I make my own. I put them down and give them names. I am allowed this. Every novelty, the door, the evening, the garden, the book in my lap. The quiet. I built it all myself.

I age another year. My life is my own. Disconsolate, beautiful. I perfume the hours. I stake claims. Who sings out from the claw of my throat? Leaves clutter my mouth, swamped and ageless. I love the horror. I forgive it, I survive it. It's always beauty and horror, meaning and meaninglessness. Woven, worm-worn knit. Thread I unspool and burnish with stars. I am held, and my arms nestle the earth. I belong here. I no longer need to speak it into being.

# *About the Author*

Haley Wooning is a writer and high school English teacher from the Bay Area. Her debut poetry collection is *Mothmouth* (Spuyten Duyvil 2019). An avid reader and puzzle lover, she also enjoys playing story-based games with her friends and community.

www.ingramcontent.com/pod-product-compliance
Lightning Source LLC
Chambersburg PA
CBHW060530080526
44586CB00012B/687